ARMED FORCES
★ ★ ★

Marine Corps

FORCE RECON

by Jack David

TORQUE™

BELLWETHER MEDIA ★ MINNEAPOLIS, MN

This edition first published in 2009 by Bellwether Media, Inc.

No part of this publication may be reproduced in whole
or in part without written permission of the publisher.
For information regarding permission, write to
Bellwether Media, Inc., Attention: Permissions Department,
Post Office Box 19349, Minneapolis, MN 55419-0349.

Library of Congress
David, Jack, 1968–
  Marine Corps Force Recon / by David Jack.
     p. cm. — (Torque. Armed forces)
  Includes bibliographical references and index.
  Summary: "Full color photography accompanies exciting
information about the Marine Corps Force Recon. The
combination of high-interest subject matter and light text is
intended for students in grades 3 through 7"—Provided by
publisher.
  ISBN-13: 978-1-60014-264-2 (hbk. : alk. paper)
  ISBN-10: 1-60014-264-8 (hbk. : alk. paper)
  1. United States. Marine Corps. Force Reconnaissance. 2.
United States. Marine Corps—Commando troops. I. Title.
  VE23.D36 2008
  359.9'64130973—dc22   2008035642

Printed in the United States of America.

CONTENTS

★ ★ ★

★ ★ ★

Chapter One

WHAT IS MARINE CORPS FORCE RECON?

The United States Marine Corps Force Recon (FORECON) is an **amphibious reconnaissance** force. These highly trained Marines specialize in gathering information about enemies both on land and in the water. The information is then used to defend the Untied States from enemy attack.

FORECON Marines go on two main kinds of missions, **green side** and **black side**. In green side missions, they secretly gather **intelligence** to help plan attacks on the enemy or prevent attacks on the United States and its allies. For example, they may find good areas for an attack or the best places for helicopters to land in enemy territory.

In black side missions, FORECON Marines carry out small attacks. They may strike key enemy locations such as bases or **airfields**. They may take over an enemy ship. These missions are usually quick, deadly, and top secret.

FORECON trainees often train alongside U.S. Navy SEALs. This specialized Navy unit focuses on fighting on sea, air, and land.

Chapter Two
WEAPONS AND GEAR

FORECON Marines need a variety of weapons to carry out their missions. The M4 **carbine** and M16 rifle are common FORECON weapons. The Marines may also carry larger machine guns, shotguns, grenade launchers, and **sniper rifles**.

Other gear protects FORECON Marines during combat. Lightweight assault vests and tough helmets protect them from most small arms fire. The helmets have built in radio gear that allows them to communicate during missions. FORECON Marines may also wear **camouflage** uniforms to help hide from the enemy.

FORECON Marines use **global positioning systems (GPS)** to find their way to specific locations. **Night-vision goggles** help them see at night. They may travel to mission sites in Desert Patrol Vehicles. These jeeps are loaded with guns and a grenade launcher. Some missions require transport in military helicopters or airplanes. These missions may require FORECON Marines to use parachutes.

Chapter Three

LIFE IN FORECON

Marines must prove that they are physically and mentally strong at a two-day **screening** before joining FORECON. They do difficult exercises to prove their fitness. They must dive 25 feet (7.6 meters) in a pool and carry up a 10-pound (4.5-kilogram) weight. They swim and tread water for long periods. They run obstacle courses. Other tests make sure Marines are intelligent and emotionally fit for service.

Those who pass the screening move on to their formal FORECON training. They study reconnaissance and learn how to gather intelligence. They train in parachuting and deep-water diving. They study and practice different styles of warfare.

FORECON Marines usually carry a small pistol, called a sidearm.

FORECON trainees learn to tie all sorts of knots. In fact, they're often called "ropers" because they have to be ready to tie specific knots in ropes at any time.

18

FORECON trainees are assigned to different specialties based on their skills and abilities. Specialties include scouting enemy territory, long-range reconnaissance, and medical care. Each unit has Marines with these skills. The Marines must work together to complete their missions.

Marines who complete all of this training then join FORECON. They're usually stationed on U.S. Navy ships. The ships take them wherever amphibious reconnaissance is needed. FORECON Marines carry out their missions in secret. When they complete a successful mission, few people ever even knew it took place.

A visit, board, search, and seizure (VBSS) mission is common for FORECON. The Marines use these four steps to take over and secure an enemy ship or boat.

GLOSSARY

★ ★ ★

airfield—an area where planes can gather, take off, and land

amphibious—able to move easily on land or in water

black side—a type of FORECON mission involving a direct action such as an attack

camouflage—made with patterns or colors that help someone blend into their surroundings

carbine—a short-barreled repeating rifle

global positioning system (GPS)—a device that uses satellites orbiting Earth to determine a precise position on the globe

green side—a type of FORECON mission involving secret reconnaissance

intelligence—information about an enemy's position, weapons, or movements

night-vision goggles—a special set of glasses that allow the wearer to see at night

reconnaissance—secret observation

screening—a selection process

sniper rifle—a rifle designed to shoot very accurately over a long distance; sniper rifles have sensitive scopes for precise aiming.

TO LEARN MORE

★ ★ ★

AT THE LIBRARY

David, Jack. *Navy SEALs*. Minneapolis, Minn.:
Bellwether, 2009.

David, Jack. *United States Marine Corps*.
Minneapolis, Minn.: Bellwether, 2008.

Sandler, Michael. *Marine Force Recon in Action*.
New York: Bearport, 2008.

ON THE WEB

Learning more about the Force Recon
is as easy as 1, 2, 3.

1. Go to www.factsurfer.com.

2. Enter "Force Recon" into the search box.

3. Click the "Surf" button and you will see a list of
    related Web sites.

With factsurfer.com, finding more information is
just a click away.

INDEX

★ ★ ★